I0753235

Actions

for Kids age 1-3

by Dayna Martin

ENGAGE BOOKS

Mailing address
PO BOX 4608
Main Station Terminal
349 West Georgia Street
Vancouver, BC
Canada, V6B 4A1

www.engagebooks.ca

Written & compiled by: Dayna Martin
Edited & designed by: A.R. Roumanis
Photos supplied by: Shutterstock

FIRST EDITION / FIRST PRINTING

LIBRARY AND ARCHIVES CANADA CATALOGUING IN PUBLICATION

Martin, Dayna, 1983–, author
Actions for kids age 1-3 / written by Dayna Martin ; edited by A.R. Roumanis.

(Engage early readers : children's learning books)
Issued in print and electronic formats.
ISBN 978-1-77226-055-7 (paperback). –
ISBN 978-1-77226-056-4 (bound). –
ISBN 978-1-77226-057-1 (pdf). –
ISBN 978-1-77226-058-8 (epub). –
ISBN 978-1-77226-059-5 (kindle)

1. Human locomotion--Juvenile literature.
I. Roumanis, A. R., editor
II. Title.

QP301.M365 2015 J612.7'6 C2015-903402-7
C2015-903403-5

Actions

for Kids age 1-3

Engage Early Readers

Children's Learning Books

By Dayna Martin

ENGAGE BOOKS / VANCOUVER

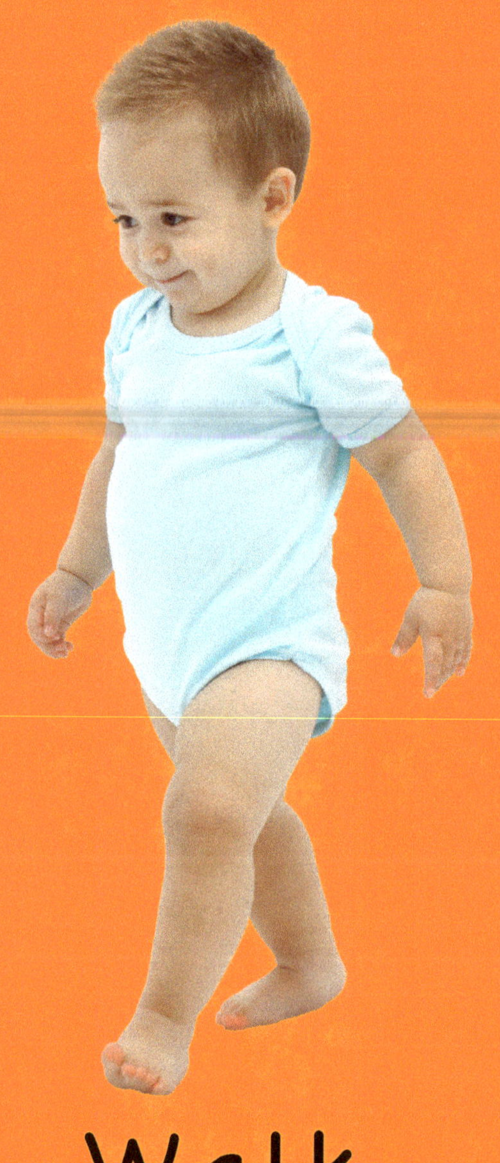

Walk

Kiss

Climb

Clap

Ride

Brush

Dive

Swim

Kick

Eat

Run

Hand Stand

Hop

Row

Pull

Pull

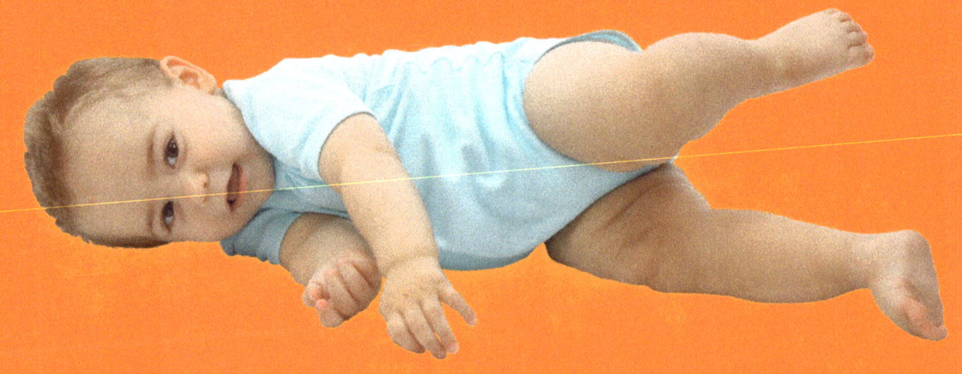

Roll

Balance

Thumbs up

Wave

Crawl

Dance

Point

Jump

Sit

Hit

Actions activity

Do you remember what these actions are called? Can you find **kick, clap, eat, crawl, hop, wave, kiss, brush,** and **ride**? Match the names to the actions below.

Answer: kiss

Answer: eat

Answer: hop

Answer: brush

Answer: kick

Answer: wave

Answer: crawl

Answer: ride

Answer: clap

age 1-3
Colors
for Kids
Yellow Fish
Orange Flower
Purple Eggplant
White Bear
Red Fire Hydrant
Blue Hat
Pink Pig

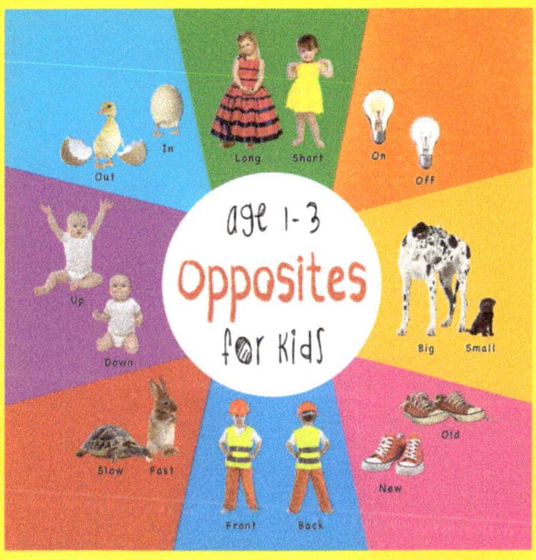
age 1-3
Opposites
for Kids
Out
In
Long
Short
On
Off
Up
Down
Big
Small
Slow
Fast
Front
Back
Old
New

age 1-3
ABCs
for Kids
Fox
Lion
Vulture
Tiger
Bear
Rabbit
Dog
Cat

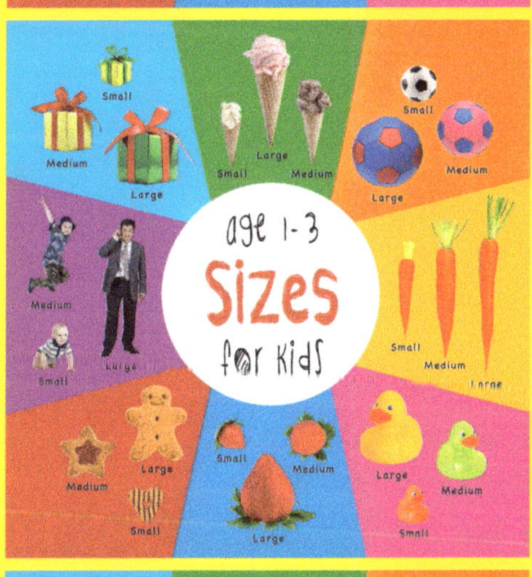
age 1-3
Sizes
for Kids
Small
Medium
Large

age 1-3
Numbers
for Kids
4 Raspberries
7 Rubber Ducks
2 Cars
8 Presents
5 Cups
1 Bowl
6 Balloons
3 Pickles

age 1-3
Emotions
for Kids
Angry
Joy
Proud
Shy
Brave
Grumpy
Shock
Fear

age 1-3
Shapes
for Kids
Starfish
Clock
Leaf
ABC
Chalkboard
Door
Rings
Cracker
Pizza

age 1-3
Sounds
for Kids
Ribbit
Moo
Vroom
Flush
Clap
Ring
Roar
Cock-a-doodle-doo

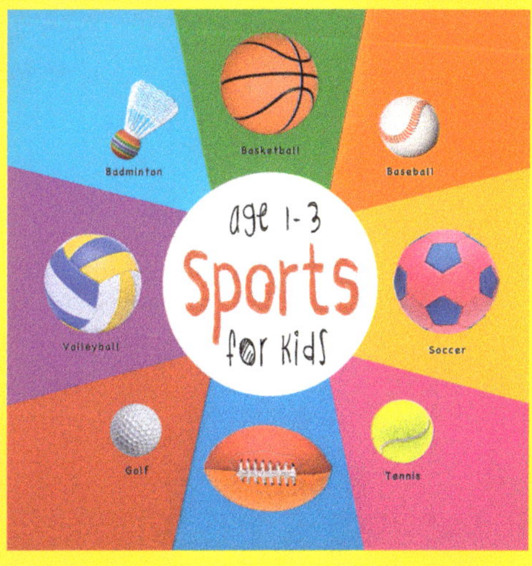
age 1-3
Sports
for Kids
Badminton
Basketball
Baseball
Volleyball
Soccer
Golf
Tennis

www.ingramcontent.com/pod-product-compliance
Lightning Source LLC
LaVergne TN
LVHW070918120826
845154LV00019BB/22

* 9 7 8 1 7 7 2 2 6 0 5 6 4 *